# Praise

"The success of every small business depends on the predictable, repeatable, daily actions taken to generate new leads, convert prospects into customers and fulfill orders in a systematized and reliable manner. What Pieter manages to achieve in *Barefoot Business* is break down what, on the face of it, can seem to be an overwhelmingly complicated endeavor, into three key systems. The implementation of which can hold the key to the success of your small business."

**Clate Mask, President and CEO, Infusion Software**

"*Barefoot Business* helps makes business simple again. Pieter has created a manual for business freedom, not just a book."

**Ash Taylor, Business Coach and Pretirement Expert**

"I've been an Infusionsoft Certified Consultant and Partner since 2011, and been working with systems and processes for a lot longer than that. Basically, I didn't think I had much to learn about systems or automation. Heck, my business is Conquer The Chaos – systems and automation is what we do! But that was before I read this book. Pieter has achieved

…and thought.

I've always found it fascinating how little most people think.

I mean properly think.

Ever since I met the author, way back in 2011, he stood out as a thinker. He sat around the table in one of my Mastermind groups alongside guys with bigger businesses, higher turnover and more profit. But no one thought more than Pieter.

He was never the loudest person in the room at those meetings, but when he spoke, we all listened. And we all paid attention because he was – always – remarkably well-thought through. And you'll see exactly what I mean once you get stuck into this book.

Pieter has a knack for seeing things the way they really are. And his wonderfully simplistic, endearing, but devastatingly straightforward, articulation of what, to him, seems obvious, has helped many hundreds of businesses within the Entrepreneurs Circle to achieve way more than they would have done without his input.

And that's what you can expect this book will do for you.

Providing you're not a dabbler.

If you're prepared to follow Pieter's instructions and read it twice, (who asks people to read their book twice!) then the insights and structures that he provides here can – and will – have a profound and deep impact on your business.

They will make you more profitable.

They will give you more time.

They will make your business more saleable. And more enjoyable.

Your customers will get a significantly improved experience which, crucially, will be consistent.

Your marketing will become properly effective and your staff more productive. Way more productive. Because that's what systems do.

This book won't win a Nobel prize. And, truthfully, it won't be a bestseller either. Because most people will miss its

But first, there are a few things to clear up: Who am I? Why should you care what I think? And why did I decide to write this book?

I am a small-business owner like you. I've never had a "real" job. I failed at school and dropped out at age 16. I eventually got a bachelor's degree in popular music performance, but I ended up as a qualified electrician running my own domestic electrical contracting business. Go figure!

I've failed in business and I've had success in business. You see, I am just like you. When I say your business is no different, pay attention. You can transform your group of court jesters into a high-performance team who will help you turn your business into a valuable asset that you could sell or hand over to a managing director so you can pursue other interests. I say this because I see it every day. I do it every day. I don't say it because we did a study in a lab or I have an MBA from a fancy school where I was taught this stuff. I say it because I've been where you are and I'd like to help you get to where you want to be.

I know what it feels like to have a million and one things to do while making sure your team is doing a million other things. You feel like you're constantly fire-fighting, never really making progress. It certainly doesn't get any easier, does it?

I wrote this book to show you how to make it easier.

Imagine...

- Focussing your energy on growing your business, not just on the next job
- Spending your time looking for new opportunities in your market, instead of simply trying to make sure something doesn't go wrong Knowing that every member of your team has the knowledge and tools they need to do a fantastic job for your customers without knocking on your door every five minutes because they don't know what to do next
- Hiring a new member of staff who contributes to your business in a meaningful way within a week, rather than still asking basic questions after six months

This is what I want to help you achieve.

Oh, and before we start, I have a confession to make: I'm obsessed with systems and processes.

Well, so what?

I know you may not be obsessed like I am – not yet, at least. But take it from me: once you start following the advice in this book, you'll fall in love with systems and you'll find a way to turn everything in your business into a process.

Let me give you an example. Every Monday morning I get an email from a little piece of software we use in our business. It says something like:

**146 tasks were completed by 14 zaps this week.**

Now, I know you might not understand what that means on a technical level, but think about this: last week, 146 things were done in my business, automatically, without me. That's 146 tasks being done every week, without taking up any of my time at all. I've set up systems and processes for them, so I don't need to think about them again. I don't have to remember to do them. I don't have to remind anyone else to do them. They just get done – day in, day out; week in, week out; month in, month out – consistently, reliably and without mistakes. I now have more time to focus on more important, higher-value things in my business.

Another reason I wrote this book is to show you the moon. I want you to see what is possible. I want to help you transform your business and, by extension, your life.

Much of the time, we are held back in life and in business not by what we do or don't *do*, but by what we do or don't *know*. Allow me to open your eyes to what is possible. And I'll show you how to achieve it, too.

You'll get real-world examples of the systems and processes we discuss in the book. And you have access to bonus material online for each chapter of the book. We live in a world that is always changing, at an ever increasing pace. It would be difficult and expensive to update this book every six months, but it's easy enough to keep the online content up to date. That means you'll always have access to the latest and greatest, no matter when you pick up this book. Simply go to www.barefootbusinessthebook.com to access the extra content.

# How to use this book

To get the most out of this book, please do the following.

1   Read it all the way through, without trying to *do* any
    of it. This will give you a glimpse of a world you may
    know little about. It will tell you some stories and give
    you some ideas, and you might even start to think
    about how to apply some of them in your business.
2   Come back and read chapters 4 to 8 again, making
    notes as you go along on what you think you can do in
    your business.
3   Start, and work backwards. It might not seem clear
    right now, but once you've gone through the book
    you'll understand that what you really need to do is
    implement the book in reverse. Confusing, I know, but
    if I wrote the book in the order you have to do it, you'd
    be even more confused and frustrated, so stick with
    me on this.

There are two key things I want you to keep in mind **all the time**. Print them off on A3 paper and stick it to your office wall if you have to, but remember...

1  **Don't get stuck on the tools**

It's tempting to start going down a rabbit hole on the detail of what to use for this or for that. Don't. I'll give you tons of information online, showing you what to use where and what might help. In the early stages of this journey though, forget about the tools. Think of it as planning a holiday. You want to go to Cape Town for a couple of weeks. You know you need to fly there, so you book a flight. What you don't do is work out exactly what you'll wear, what you'll have for breakfast at the airport, what type of aeroplane you'll be on, and so on. You simply book a flight and work out the details later. The same applies here. First, we'll work out what systems and processes you need in your business (hint: there are only three main systems, no matter what business you're in). And then we'll work out what you need to make it happen.

2  **Make little bets**

When you first start applying what you learn here, make little bets. Don't start by getting rid of everything you have and trying to transform every aspect of your business overnight. That will hurt and be disruptive, and it might even kill your business. Like DIY healthcare, it's OK to start doing exercise and changing your diet based on what you read in a book or see on the internet. But you wouldn't use the same approach if you needed a heart bypass.

Having said that, the most important thing to do is to **start**. Once you get started, you'll soon get into it and start feeling like an expert at this – which you will be, among your peers.

Your first efforts will be short term. They may seem great at first, but as you learn more you will find that you need to change or completely redesign them. That's fine – it's the best bit about this. Nothing is set in stone, and you can always improve. Just focus on this principle:

You can only improve a system that actually exists. If there's no system, there's nothing to improve!

Which leads me to a word of warning:

**You still have to do the most important work.**

Let me give you a couple of examples.

One of the services we provide our clients is a lead-generation machine, where we take care of all the lead generation. All they have to do is follow up the leads and make sales. This makes some customers think that it's all done for them and the business will just happen. This is not the case.

A well-designed lead-generation machine will make your phone ring and bring enquiries in, but you need a reliable client-acquisition system to turn those leads into business.

Putting the right systems and automation in place won't leave you with nothing to do but count your money. What is does is free up your time so you can do the most important work: **sell**.

We recently launched a new lead-generation machine for a client, and the early results were encouraging. But they also highlighted an issue, and not for the first time.

After setting the system live and generating ten enquiries in the first twenty-four hours (cost per lead – £3.50, average transaction value – £1,200) it became clear that the business owner was not responding to any of the enquiries. The customer was afraid of interfering with what we were doing.

Somehow, in engaging us to take over the digital marketing and lead generation, our customer abdicated responsibility for the new enquiries coming in. My obvious response was to get in touch with everybody right away. Yes, we can put some automated follow-up emails in place, but these are mainly for people who enquire via the website late at night.

The psychology at play here is fascinating, and we see it more often than we should.

A business owner explains that they need more leads in their business, and when those leads turn up, what happens? They keep themselves busy with the work of the business instead of turning those leads into happy customers.

This situation reminded me of a comment that Daniel Priestley (www.keypersonofinfluence.com) once made in reply to a question. The question itself is not important here, but the answer has universal importance for every business owner. Here's what Daniel said:

*"It's worthwhile to remove all expectation that business should come to you and you won't need to sell yourself. Ferrari isn't the go-to brand for sports cars: they sell Ferraris. Google has armies of people selling AdWords campaigns. Rolex train their people to sell watches. Growing a business will always require a sales approach that generates enough business. Being a key person of influence doesn't remove the need to sell, it gives you more opportunities to sell."*

That is such a simple and crucial point.

If you have any reservations about selling or if you're hiding behind your email auto-responder, print out the above quote and put it on your wall.

No matter what great, inexpensive technology you have available, no matter what industry you are in or how big or small your business is, you need to sell.

Sell!

It's a verb. It's something you have to do, not something that happens.

Please don't spend your time working on everything I discuss in this book at the expense of serving your clients and moving your business forward.

# CHAPTER ONE

# Barefoot Business – Why?

The questions I am asked most about developing systems and processes for small businesses fall into two clear camps:

1. Why should I do it? Why should I prioritise it over everything else I have to do?
2. How do I do it? Where do I even start?

The second camp is the main focus of this book, so before we get into that I'll answer the first group of questions.

Why?

The short answer is that having efficient and effective systems and processes in your business makes life easier and better. And it can massively increase the value of your business. But I know that sounds simplistic and you might not really believe me yet. I also know that as business owners we want to know detail. Who? What? When? Where? How? Why?

Let me tell you a bit about myself by way of example.

The title of this book, *Barefoot Business*, is all about what my own systems and processes allow me to do.

I grew up in South Africa, which you might have gathered from my name. (No, I am not in any way related to any of the famous South African rugby or cricket players. De Villiers is a common surname in South Africa, a bit like Smith in England.)

I grew up in an era when everyone walked to school and back. I'd seldom get far from the school gates before taking my shoes off for the walk home. I'd far rather carry a pair of shoes than wear them. I am never as relaxed as I am when walking around barefoot, and it's still the first thing I do when I get home from a meeting or anywhere else that demands a pair of shoes.

One of my little pleasures is walking around our local village with my daughters, all three of us barefoot. Everyone stares as if nobody else has feet!

**For me, the main tangible result of having systems and processes set up for my business is that it allows me to take my shoes off more often.**

For you, there will be something else that you value – something that will become an everyday occurrence, easy to fit into your busy life, once your business is properly systemised and all your processes are defined.

Let's look at the direct impact on your business, and why systems and processes are so powerful.

## Increased productivity

Having all your systems in place allows your employees to get on and do their jobs. They know what to do every day, and they know how to do it.

When an enquiry comes in, there are several fixed options. All that needs to happen is for the enquiry to be funnelled down the correct channel, and the rest is then controlled and predictable.

Think about a car production line.

The Porsche 911 has been an icon since 1963. In June 2015 alone Porsche sold more than 21,000 of them. And Porsche is only able to churn out that many cars in one year because of systems and processes. Not only that, but there are twenty-two different engines for the 911, and you can have it painted any colour you like, increasing the complexity by an order of magnitude.

But because Porsche designed the production line first, allowing for all the elements that are the same on every 911, they only really need to deal with the margins of difference. They don't build every car from scratch, only the customised elements.

It's the same in every business, including yours. There are always certain milestones – things every customer has to receive or experience. This is where to start developing your systems.

Before you say, "But Porsche has millions and millions of dollars to spend, and I am not in manufacturing," here's an example on a smaller scale: a local kitchen design and installation company.

When I first met the couple who run this business, they were really struggling. They were working seven days a week, fourteen to eighteen hours a day. They had no life outside their business and they felt imprisoned – hating the daily grind that was just keeping everything afloat.

We spent some time going through the details of their business, from the moment the phone rings or someone walks into their showroom to the flowers they leave behind once a job is finished.

It was a mess, because there was no defined system. Everyone had their own way of doing things, and every job was carried out as if it was the first.

With my help, they were able to break down their entire business into eight discrete milestones or stages of a project. They defined every bit of chaos they would usually have in the office and on-site as belonging in one of the eight stages. And this made it easy to assign responsibility and start to track performance.

As you can imagine, this relatively simple work transformed their business. It also let them hand over some of the responsibility to their staff, because everyone now knew what to do and how to manage the projects.

What fancy technology did we use to achieve this massive shift in their business? Cardboard folders, a checklist and eight pigeonholes. That's how high-tech it needed to be.

The positive impact that this had on productivity was immediate, and it was huge.

Everyone can now see at a glance what stage a project is in and what tasks are outstanding.

This results in less internal communication, fewer customer-service calls and a general reduction in chaos. Everything is now under control and everyone knows what to do next.

Remember what I said: don't get stuck on the tools!

## Reducing cost

In most businesses, the highest overhead walks on two legs. If you want to grow your business, you can't do it on your own. You need a team. But the majority of businesses hire overqualified staff, who then need to be paid what they think they're worth.

Hiring a great team is important and the right thing to do, but only if you first create an environment for them to contribute to their highest ability.

Think about McDonald's. They are able to run a multi-billion-dollar monster while mainly employing "minimum-wage kids" who usually can't be bothered to tidy their bedrooms. McDonald's doesn't hire qualified chefs to work in its restaurants.

The only reason McDonald's is able to do this is that they use clearly defined systems and processes. And that is the key here: **clearly defined**. Not just "make it up as you go along".

Another great example is a chain of sandwich shops, Pret A Manger. These guys are the ultimate at systems and processes, and they sell egg sandwiches!

Every Pret store has, on-site, the complete, documented systems and processes for **everything** in the business. When you start working for them, you go on training for two weeks. Two weeks of training to make sandwiches and coffee! How much training did the last person you hired get before they were unleashed on your customers?

Pret has three or four pages dedicated to how to sweep the floor outside the shop, complete with diagrams and instructions.

That is why in 2015 they made profits of over £84 million from selling egg sandwiches.

For these two businesses and many more like them, their distinct advantage over the also-rans is their clearly defined systems and processes.

Here's an example of how systems affect cost:

> Let's say you identify a two-minute task in your business. Every business is filled with "It only takes two minutes" tasks. If one of these tasks is performed ten times a day, that's twenty minutes; if it is done by two members of staff, that's forty minutes. It doesn't seem much to be bothered about, does it?
>
> But if you're open five days a week and you do business for fifty weeks of the year, that's now 8,000 minutes – or more than two whole working weeks – spent on this two-minute task. Even if your staff are only paid the highest national minimum wage of £7.50 per hour (UK – 2017), you'll spend minimum £1,000 every year on getting a simple two-minute task done. What if you found ten of these tasks throughout your business? Or twenty? If you were to automate them, or completely eliminate them, by sorting out your

systems, you could have £10,000 to £20,000 additional profit every year to reinvest in your business. Now can you see how vital this is to your business?

## Complete integration

The way to deal with these two-minute tasks, which spread like a cancer across your business, is complete integration. I'll use another massive company to get the point across, and then I'll show you how it works in a small business.

Take any supermarket. These guys have hundreds if not thousands of outlets, dealing with millions and millions of individual transactions every year. How successful would they be if their systems were not integrated, but were standalone islands requiring manual intervention?

When you use the self-checkout at your local supermarket, nobody needs to collect the receipt and keep it in a shoebox until the end of the week, when the bookkeeper comes round and enters all the receipts onto a spreadsheet, which is then sent to the accountant for the tax returns, et cetera.

The moment you complete your transaction, its details are sent automatically to the accounting software, while at the same time the local store's stock position is updated for the items you bought. A large supermarket chain could not function without this level of integration. Even if they found a way to avoid integration, they would spend so much money on staffing all the separate departments that they could never compete with the systemised and integrated competitor down the road.

It's the same for you.

Just imagine your business is in a position where you can do the same amount of business, or even more, but you need one employee less. That saving goes straight to your bottom line.

Here's an example.

> I do a lot of work with a family-run window-shutter and blind company.
>
> I designed and implemented complete systems and processes for them, integrating their customer-relationship management (CRM), website, Facebook, admin, operations and accounting functions. As a result, they've moved from a situation where everyone

was busy running around and working long hours, to a situation where one director (first generation) has been able to move into an advisory role and pursue other interests and the two remaining directors (second generation) have stepped away almost completely from the day-to-day tasks. They can now focus on growing the business and making strategic decisions instead of dealing with the project-by-project decisions of doing business.

They achieved all this while almost doubling their turnover and reducing their costs by about 35%.

## Training

Taking on new employees is one of the most costly investments any business owner can make. You have to pay their wages, manage them day to day and train them to do their job. It can often take three to six months for a new member of staff to become productive and start adding to the bottom line. That's a long time to wait.

Now, think about McDonald's again. Do you think they wait three to six months before they expect a staff member to know how to do their job? No. You shouldn't have to either.

By having clearly defined systems and processes, you can greatly reduce the time it takes for a new member of staff to get up to speed.

The ideal is to create an integrated system. The business system tells the employee what to do and when. Then, the online standard operation procedures (SOPs) tell them exactly how to do it.

There should never be a situation where John learns from Sally, Jenny learns from John and Mike learns from Jenny. This creates chaos and everyone will do everything slightly differently. If everyone learns from the SOPs and follows the systems you put in place, you'll have created a machine inside your business that gives you an invisible and distinct advantage over your competition.

The basic premise is:

**the system runs the business; the staff run the system.**

I am sure that some, if not all, of the above has given you plenty of motivation and proof that, wherever possible, you should systemise and automate your business.

Now you know that, let's get stuck in and look at the key systems every business needs. Don't worry if you feel overwhelmed; you need to focus on three systems only.

# CHAPTER TWO

# The Three Key Systems

As with many things in life, when we are right up against it we are unable to see overarching themes or trends. It is the same with your business, and every business ever created.

When you're inside your business, working from day to day, you can be easily convinced that your business is made up of hundreds or thousands of different parts that all need to work in order for the business to run.

The flaw in this (lack of) perspective is two-fold.

First, your business is not really made up of hundreds or thousands of parts. And second, the parts that do exist in your business shouldn't just all work; they should all work **together**. The aim is complete integration. Having different sections of your business operate in isolation, with no real integration or communication between the parts, is a sure-fire recipe for low productivity and wasted time and money – if you're lucky. Or, if you're not, for disaster and chaos!

Once you make the time to step back from your business and get an overview of the whole, without the day-to-day focus on the minutiae, you will see the three key systems that make up your business. In fact, they're the same three systems for every business on the planet.

It's like looking at a painting. If you look at it from two inches away, you can't tell what the overall picture is. You can see thousands of brush-strokes, fine detail in colour mixes and tiny imperfections. But, no matter how you move around the canvas, you never get a sense of what the picture actually looks like.

Once you step away from the canvas and look at it from a greater distance, you suddenly see the entire picture. You are able to spot certain focal points and themes, all of which were missing when you were right up close.

And so it is with your business.

No matter what business you are in, there are only three primary systems to develop and focus on.

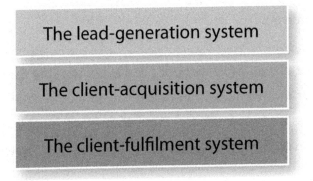

Once you have these three key systems in place, fully integrated, with as much automation as possible, you have a business that sits on strong foundations, with a real structure in place. And while there are other, peripheral systems, such as staff recruitment and management, the three listed above are the most important and valuable for you right now.

With these three systems in place, your business has a concrete and tangible advantage over your competitors. While they scramble around not knowing where the next customer is coming from or wondering how to get their team working together, you will be in a position to see at a glance what business is in the pipeline. You'll have key performance indicators at your fingertips. Like a Formula One racing driver or a fighter-jet pilot, you'll have all the right dials in front of you, allowing you to adjust to the circumstances around you.

Above all, you will have built a real asset. You'll be the proud owner of a business that doesn't need you in order to be successful. Your business – your team – will be able to deal with everything that comes along, because of the systems.

Here's an example from the world of sport.

> The All Blacks (New Zealand's rugby team) is arguably the most successful team of all time, in any sport.
>
> The key to their success is their systems.
>
> New Zealand has a system throughout the country of nurturing and developing young talent. (This is their **lead-generation system**.)
>
> The team itself has a longstanding, unique training regime. Everything is done deliberately to ensure the best team possible, both physically and tactically. (This is their **client-acquisition system**.)
>
> Then we come to their greatest advantage over every team they face. They have a plan and system of play that they execute with complete focus. (This is their **client-fulfilment system**.)
>
> The All Blacks don't seem to care who the team on

the other side of the field is. They turn up with a plan and they execute it, time and again.

They are able to do this because every member of the team has a defined role and responsibility. Every team member knows exactly what is expected of him. More importantly, every team member is equipped to fulfil his role within the team, with complete support from every other member of the team.

Can you imagine the chaos on a rugby field if every player just ran around after the ball, with no fixed role or position? How successful would the All Blacks be if everyone turned up for training only when it suited them, or if there was nothing in place to develop new players for the team who will play in the World Cup five or six years from now?

What are you doing today, to ensure you have the clients you need next year?

This is how you should look at your business and the team you have around you. Are you selecting the best team members for each position? Does every team member know what is expected of them in every situation? Do you provide them with everything they need to succeed?

Before we go into the details and examples of each of the three key systems, here's a quick overview of each.

## Lead-generation system

If cash flow is the lifeblood of every business, a constant stream of new leads is the oxygen.

Don't confuse your lead-generation system with new sales, though. This is not its function. The lead-generation system has two simple components:

1 Ways for your prospects to raise their hand and say "I am interested in what you sell"
2 A way for you to capture their details and note their interest

It really is no more complicated than that. Provided your lead-generation system performs these two functions – and, crucially, can hand all these leads over to a client-acquisition system – you can start to predict future revenue.

## Client-acquisition system

The focus here is solely on your first transaction with each client. Depending on the market you are in, this could be a one-off transaction or the start of plenty of repeat business. But the focus remains the same – secure the first transaction; receive the first transfer of money in exchange for the value you provide.

## Client-fulfilment system

Here is where you need to shine like the All Blacks. One of their recent heroes, Dan Carter, the highest ever point-scorer in rugby has a jaw-dropping 89% win rate with the team. And the real achievement is that the All Blacks have created an environment where a single player can score that many points.

Does the delivery of your core product or service (fulfilment) have an 89% success rate with your customers? If you don't have a well-defined and developed client-fulfilment system in your business, you are making it up as you go along on every job. True success and value comes from having a defined, repeatable system in place that ensures replacements, reworks or refunds are the rare exceptions.

Let's move on to the next chapter, where we'll look at the lead-generation system in more detail.

# CHAPTER THREE

# Your Lead-Generation System

The success measure of your lead-generation system is whether it provides your business with a constant flow of new enquiries.

These people will not necessarily buy from you the moment they discover your business. Your lead-generation system is a mechanism that allows people at different stages of the prospect matrix to raise their hand and show interest in what you are selling. This gives them an extremely low commitment threshold – in some cases, no direct commitment at all. That is, your lead-generation system is not intended to get people buying from you the moment they find you.

## Prospect matrix

All prospects fall somewhere on the line between not realising they have a problem and desperately wanting a solution to a pressing matter.

37

At the same time, they fall somewhere between not knowing you exist and trusting that you are the only and obvious solution to their problem. (See the following diagram)

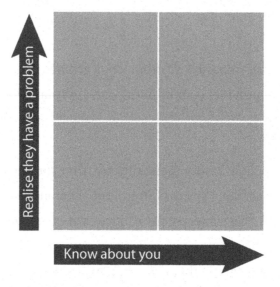

This means you have to find ways to catch people at all the possible combination points on the matrix.

If you simply focus on the people who don't know you exist and don't know they have a problem, which requires **interrupt marketing**, such as Facebook, you'll find that every sale is hard work and full of objections. At the other end of the spectrum, you might find someone who knows they have a problem but doesn't know you exist, which requires **search network marketing** (Google, Bing, Yahoo, et cetera).

I've plotted these two scenarios in the matrix below. It is clear that we are leaving large swathes of prospects out with this simplistic approach.

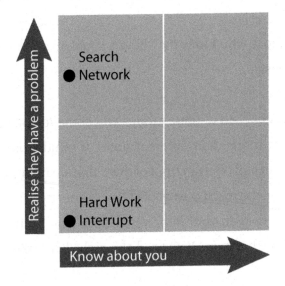

A fully developed lead-generation machine should cover the whole prospect matrix.

The four main groups to target are (bear with me on this!):

1 Those who **don't know** they have a problem and **don't know** you exist
2 Those who **don't know** they have a problem but **know** you exist
3 Those who **know** they have a problem but **don't know** you exist
4 Those who **know** they have a problem and **know** you exist

Prospects in each of these groups will come to your door at different times and in different states of mind. You need to put content and offers in front of them that are right for where they are on the matrix. To quote Dan S Kennedy, "If you want to attract deer to your back yard, there's no point putting cheese on the lawn. You need the right bait for the right critter."

In essence, your lead-generation system creates an "all roads lead to Rome" scenario. Different prospects will find you in different ways, at different times. All these forms of raising their hand lead to the same door into your client-acquisition system, which we'll look at in the next chapter.

Let's look at some examples of lead-generation systems.

Please keep the following in mind when you read the examples in the remainder of this book. Your job is not to find opportunities to say "Well, that's great, but my business is different." Believe me, having worked with hundreds of businesses, I can assure you that yours is no different. Your job is to start sowing the seeds of change by asking yourself "How will that work in my business?"

We'll start with a basic example. Systems don't have to be complex.

Our first example is a window-shutter company, The Scottish Shutter Company (SSC).

SSC's product lends itself to beautiful "before and after" photographs of rooms with old curtains and then new shutters in place. The photos are taken in nice houses, which stirs the prospect's aspirational emotions.

The ideal prospect is on the matrix where they know they have a problem; for example, they are redecorating or refurbishing their home. Ideally, they also know that SSC is Scotland's premier window-shutter supplier.

The problem SSC had to overcome is that they have no real way of knowing when someone is about to refurbish their home. For example, looking at local planning applications would only cover a fraction of the available opportunities. So SSC needed to find a way of letting prospects know about the company and have them express an interest.

This system is based on a simple five-image Facebook ad, targeted at SSC's ideal customer avatar. This allows SSC to appear repeatedly in front of people who are much like their best customers.

The ad does not offer the product for sale or at a reduced rate. The response needs to be a low commitment from the prospect's perspective. At this point, SSC is not trying to determine that a prospect is ready to buy, only that they have an interest in the product. The Facebook ad simply offers viewers the option to download a brochure. All the prospect needs to do is tell SSC where to email the brochure.

There is a second step in this little system, though. Once the person has given their email address, they are given an option to request a nice glossy, printed copy of the same brochure. The benefit of doing this is two-fold.

For one, SSC now has the potential customer's name, email and postal address – all extremely useful when passed to their client-acquisition system.

SSC also has something physical placed in the prospect's house, which is much more likely to be looked at again than the PDF sent by email. This brochure is also likely to stay on the coffee table or in the magazine rack for quite some time.

As far as the lead-generation system is concerned – mission accomplished!

Some lead-generation systems need to be much more complex than this for the subsequent client-acquisition system to be effective.

Let's look at a client of mine who works in private investment. I'll keep this anonymous to protect sensitive information.

The client's lead-generation system here has three main purposes:

1 Generate interest
2 Give a reminder (if required)
3 Gather information.

Step one (generating interest) is a simple Facebook or Google Display ad, which suggests an article, written by the client, based on the most pressing financial or political issues of the day. This joins the conversation in the prospect's mind.

This ad does not offer anything for sale: a sale here could be worth over £50,000, so it will require more than a simple ad. The ad just leads to an extensive, topic-specific article.

The article is quite lengthy and has two main objectives:

1 To educate the prospect.
2 To position the author as an expert and authority.

In the sidebar and the footer of the page displaying the article, the prospect is presented with the option to complete a survey to help them determine where they are on their investment journey and how financially independent they are.

This appears on the page multiple times in a colour that stands out from the rest of the design.

Should the prospect decide to take the survey, they bypass step two and go straight to step three.

We'll look at step two (the reminder) first, though.

This is again a Facebook or Google Display ad, which is used for **remarketing**.

What remarketing allows you to do is show relevant ads, in Facebook and Google Display, **only** to people who have already visited your website or certain pages on your website.

You will only ever see this ad if you clicked on the ad that took you to the article.

The function of this ad is simply to remind the prospect to go and take the survey. We know they saw the survey advertised on the article page, so we can simply remind them to go and do it.

Step three (gathering information) is the survey, which is the main focus of this particular lead-generation machine.

The survey is a set of multiple-choice questions about the prospect's investing habits and experience and their financial aims for the future. The information gathered here is fed into the client-acquisition system and used to create a **unique universe** for each prospect. More on that in the next chapter.

If you're thinking that asking people for their personal financial information will scare them off, you're right. This particular lead-generation system combats the problem in two ways.

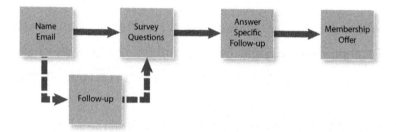

First, the survey asks for the person's name and email address before presenting any questions. This allows the investment organisation to follow up with anyone who does not complete the survey, building a relationship of trust that will lead the prospect to feel safe and confident enough to complete the survey.

The other function of these questions is to repel people. Not everyone can become your customer. You only want to work with your ideal customers, and hurdles like this survey are a means of filtering out those who are not ready to work with you.

## The key to any lead-generation system

Two factors are crucial to the success of your lead-generation system:

1  **It must never stop.** Your lead-generation machine must continuously feed new prospects into your business. Not just on some days, and not just when you remember to do it. This leads to the second crucial factor.

2  **It needs to be a fully integrated system.** You shouldn't have to be reminded to turn it on or get it going on a Monday morning. And it should plug straight into your client-acquisition system.

# CHAPTER FOUR

# The Client Acquisition System

The client-acquisition system is where you get the chance to create a truly unique universe for every prospect who knocks on your door, without the chaos of making it up as you go along.

We'll stick with our two examples from the previous chapter: one, a blinds and shutters company, the other a high-net-worth investor membership organisation. I'll also throw in some examples of what other businesses do, but the two main ones will give you a good view of the client-acquisition system for an online and a bricks-and-mortar business. Remember, your business is **not** different!

The key to the success of your client-acquisition system is segmentation. Your customers are different and you should address them and communicate with them appropriately.

Here's a trivial example of this not being done. Before we had any children, my wife and I lived in a first-floor flat, but we still got calls from conservatory salesmen. Relatively simple segmentation of their list would have saved their sales staff loads of time and allowed them to focus on people who would might have needed their product.

The same applies to your business, and to every business. First, find out what the key differences are. Then, match your offers to each prospect's requirements.

These can be simple to begin with. For example, I built a system for a gym in the UK and their first, and most obvious, segmentation was gender. Men and women tend to train for different reasons and have different motivations.

Beyond these two groups, they segmented their audience as follows:

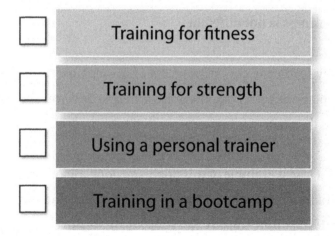

Simply paying attention to these segments of their audience, and addressing them accordingly, has had a massive impact on the message sent out to each of these groups. You might need to do more work to begin with to get this right, but the rewards are massive for all businesses that segment effectively.

## Creating unique universes

Did you ever read those *Choose Your Own Adventure* books when you were a child? I loved them. Instead of reading the book from beginning to end, the reader chooses from options that take them on their own journey through the book and lead to different endings. I probably paid more attention to finding out what led where and how the books actually work than I did to reading the stories. I suppose that's not surprising, considering my obsession with systems!

This is exactly what you want to create for your prospects. Let them go on a journey with your business and allow them to control that journey, or at least feel as if they control it.

The most basic example of this is the first-name merge field in any email newsletter or auto-responder system. You can send the same email to ten people, but they each see their own name at the top.

That is the most basic unique universe you can create. Nobody pays attention to it any more, because it's become taken for granted, but it gives you an idea of what I mean.

A good analogy to keep in mind when designing your universes is getting from A to B. Let's say we both need to get to Birmingham.

I would drive from my house down the A3 to join the M25 at junction 10, and then continue on the M25 until junction 16, where I'd join the M40. I'd stay on the M40 until I joined the M42 around junction 15. Depending on where I was going in Birmingham, I'd get off the M42 at junction 5 or 6.

For you, unless you happen to live around the corner from me, the journey would be different. You might not drive at all. You might be in New York, where you get a flight to Birmingham International Airport, then a train to Birmingham New Street.

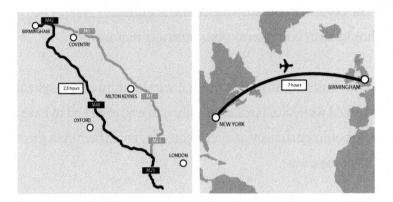

Now, we both had to reach the same destination, but our journeys had nothing in common. If you were given the directions to Birmingham that I followed, you'd have had no chance of getting there – you'd have had to research it yourself and find your own way.

But this is exactly what business owners do every day. They give all their prospects the same directions, no matter where they are starting from or how far they have to travel. And they wonder why some get lost along the way!

The front end of your client-acquisition system should allow your prospect to indicate to you where they are on the prospect matrix. You can then lead them through a unique universe to the point where they are ready to buy from you.

How complex should your client-acquisition system be? It should be as complex as your business requires.

For my business, 48 Hour Launch, I started with a simple system. I worked with local businesses only, and everyone had to have a ninety-minute strategy session before they could become a client. The process was:

That worked really well. It became more complex only when I developed the business and added products and services.

The same should happen in your business. Start with a simple system. Test it and develop it. Don't wait until you've designed the perfect system before you start to use it. If you do that, you'll never have a system in your business.

Remember, unless you have a system, you can't improve it.

## Example unique universes

Let's look at a bricks-and-mortar business first. We'll use SSC from the previous chapter.

SSC's client-acquisition system starts with a manual email response from the office.

Their lead-generation system produces up to 600 leads a month, so how do they cope with this?

The short answer is they don't. At the end of their lead-generation system, prospects must request a quote online or request a time-limited discount code. These are the keys to the door of the client-acquisition system.

Trying to sell to all these leads at this stage would be like one member of staff standing at the door of McDonald's trying to ask everyone who walks past what they would like for lunch. But they have a system – you have to walk up to the counter.

Once the manual email has been sent, the system knows and the prospect moves into the information-gathering stage of the client-acquisition system. This is a key milestone for all prospect journeys. Without all the required information, SSC can't give you an estimate, so you cannot progress.

What happens inside the information-gathering stage? It doesn't matter. It could take the form of emails, phone calls and so on. How many calls and emails depends on the prospect, but the key is that all the required information is gathered.

Looking at our driving analogy again, to get to Birmingham I don't need to know whether I'll drive in the fast lane or the slow lane or whether I'm going to stop for a coffee on the way: that's up to me. What is not up to me is where Birmingham is. My end destination is fixed, but the rest feels completely up to me; I feel in control.

This is how it will be for your staff when they are working in the system in your business: controlled freedom.

Driving is not at all like going somewhere by train. The station locations are fixed, the track is fixed and the stops in between are fixed. Even if I don't want to go a particular way, I have no freedom or control. The train is leaving at a certain time, and I have to make sure I am there.

Many people think that having systems and processes in place means they are building a railway system, rigid and fixed. This is not the case at all.

The aim is to build a flexible transport network where your prospect gets to choose the route, even though the final destination is fixed.

Let's have a look at a much more complicated client-acquisition system to give you an idea of what is actually possible.

Again, don't get stuck on asking "How on earth do I do this?" Keep an open mind and try to look for ways you can use the strategy in your business. We'll look at the technical aspects later.

If you recall the high-net-worth investor membership business mentioned earlier, the aim of their lead-generation system is to get the prospect to take an online survey.

We'll dig a little deeper now into what happens the moment you complete the survey. This part will get a little complicated, but stay with me.

You will find a complete video walkthrough of this client-acquisition system at www.barefootbusinessthebook.com.

The survey is made up of six questions: SQ1 to SQ6.

The questions are all multiple choice. With the exception of SQ6, you can choose only one answer for each question.

So, using the question labels shown above, when you complete the survey you are "tagged" in the CRM system according to the answers you gave. For example, your profile could be tagged as follows:

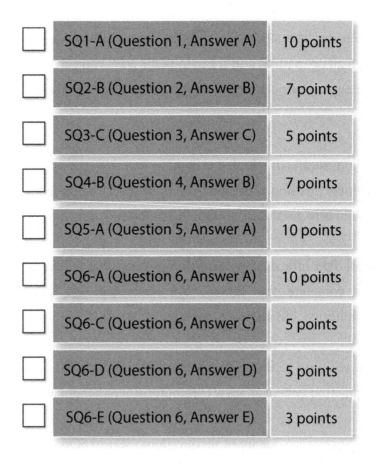

| | | |
|---|---|---|
| ☐ | SQ1-A (Question 1, Answer A) | 10 points |
| ☐ | SQ2-B (Question 2, Answer B) | 7 points |
| ☐ | SQ3-C (Question 3, Answer C) | 5 points |
| ☐ | SQ4-B (Question 4, Answer B) | 7 points |
| ☐ | SQ5-A (Question 5, Answer A) | 10 points |
| ☐ | SQ6-A (Question 6, Answer A) | 10 points |
| ☐ | SQ6-C (Question 6, Answer C) | 5 points |
| ☐ | SQ6-D (Question 6, Answer D) | 5 points |
| ☐ | SQ6-E (Question 6, Answer E) | 3 points |

Each answer has been given a point weighting, which allows the investment business to add the points up and give you a score out of 100. The example above gives a score of 62/100.

The business uses this score to decide what email response you will receive. The system is set up to choose from five emails, depending on which range your score lies in:

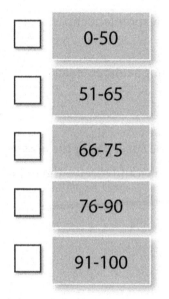

In this way, the business can speak to a person with a score of 95 in a tone that acknowledges that they are an experienced and accomplished investor. At the other end of the spectrum, the business can address someone with a score of 45 as a beginner.

This alone is already more than most businesses are willing or able to do.

Read that sentence again. Having these systems and processes in place puts you well in front of your competitors.

The investment business wasn't satisfied, though. They wanted to address every question on the survey, in relation to the answers the respondent chose.

They do this by having a unique email for every answer to every question.

If you completed the survey with the answers outlined in the example above, you would receive the following emails:

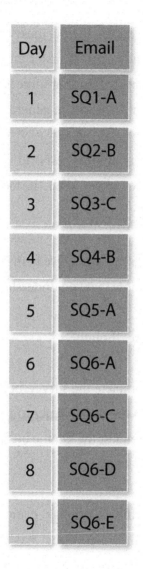

| Day | Email |
| --- | --- |
| 1 | SQ1-A |
| 2 | SQ2-B |
| 3 | SQ3-C |
| 4 | SQ4-B |
| 5 | SQ5-A |
| 6 | SQ6-A |
| 7 | SQ6-C |
| 8 | SQ6-D |
| 9 | SQ6-E |

Are you still with me? I hope so.

Why would we do this? Why does it work?

This type of system allows the business owner to build up a level of trust and authority far faster and on a deeper level than would be possible by sending some generic emails about the business or about investors in general.

Here, the business is able to respond specifically to each answer the prospect gave. Well, it feels specific to the prospect.

What you are attempting to achieve here is to show your level of expertise and to show that you understand your customers.

It does not stop there, though.

The moment you complete the survey, before you receive any emails you are given the opportunity to request an Investor's Survival Kit. If you request the kit, the business sends an email with three download links.

Please note, and this is crucial: every email and every download you send to a prospect has to provide massive value. This is not a case of bait and switch. Bait and switch is a technique that was used widely in the early days of AdWords, where, for example, an insurance company would bid on or place an ad for a particular car. You search for the car and see the ad, but when you click on the ad, they try to sell you insurance, not a car.

You must truly help your prospects before they become a customer.

As Frank Kern says, "The best way to show someone how you can help them in the future is to help them now."

Once you request the Investor's Survival Kit, you are given the chance to apply to join the membership club, at which point you are sent a box of goodies in the post.

## Track everything: learn to love data

The other aspect of your client-acquisition system will be collecting and tracking all the data you need to ensure your prospects have the best experience on their way to becoming customers.

An example of this can be taken from SSC.

SSC's client-acquisition system involves the following key milestones:

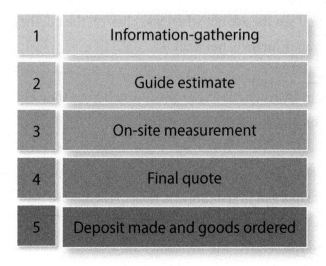

| 1 | Information-gathering |
|---|---|
| 2 | Guide estimate |
| 3 | On-site measurement |
| 4 | Final quote |
| 5 | Deposit made and goods ordered |

They have built a personal and effective detail into their system.

When team members go out to measure on-site, they complete drawings and forms with all the details and measurements, so they can design the final product and place the order.

The genius is that at the same time they note down whether there is a pet dog, and, if yes, what the dog's name is.

Why?

At SSC, they have two dogs in their showroom. So, the day after the measure was completed a parcel arrives at the prospect's house.

This parcel is actually a gift from Lottie, one of the

SSC dogs, to the prospect's dog, with a nice card. The prospect always comments on this, and it shows the level of attention that SSC pays to detail. The prospect is assured that they are in safe hands.

Again, the key here is not that it happens every now and again, but that it happens every time. It is part of the system.

How many times after you have given a prospect a quote or proposal do you get in touch with them? Is every prospect who walks through your door today ready to buy?

Most of the prospects who you meet this week will not be ready to buy. Just because they don't buy today or this week doesn't mean they don't *want* to buy.

I used to run a smart-home and audio-visual installation business. I knew that on average, it would take five months from a first enquiry to an order. After that, it could be another four or five months before we got on-site and started the work.

The prospects wanted to buy when they first called, but they couldn't. Most of them were builders or in the process of moving or renovating and didn't yet have any walls for us to hang TVs on.

If I had simply given up after the first couple of months, I would have missed out on a lot of business. It was never the prospect's job to remember to do business with us. We had to remind them repeatedly that we were still here and happy to do business with them when they were ready.

The only reason we knew how long it took on average to get a sale was that we tracked all the data in the business and learned from it.

Whether your data is a dog's name or the average timescale for a transaction, track the data in your business. The data is there even when you don't track it; it's just not available to you in a way that allows you to improve the relationships you build with your prospects and customers.

## Follow-up, follow-up, follow-up

Data is even more useful when you decide how to follow up with prospects and customers.

One of the businesses I set up sells tartan scarves and stoles. We could run some ads every year to make sales in the lead-up to and during winter. But our sales would be much lower, and so would our income, simply because we were lazy.

Instead, we follow up, using content that is targeted to specific prospects and past customers. Again, this is all possible because we track the data on the first and every sale.

Let's use the scarves as an example.

If you bought a Royal Stewart scarf from me, you would eventually receive follow-up offers on all of the items shown below:

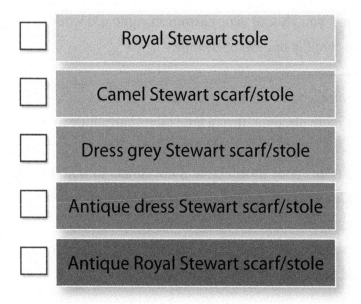

☐ Royal Stewart stole

☐ Camel Stewart scarf/stole

☐ Dress grey Stewart scarf/stole

☐ Antique dress Stewart scarf/stole

☐ Antique Royal Stewart scarf/stole

These are specific to what you bought in the past. I can even refer to your purchase and include a picture of what you bought in the email. By doing this, I will stand out from all the other retailers because I remembered and made you feel special.

## Put your best offer on the table first

Many businesses take the view that they need to get as much money out of the first transaction as possible. This might be true if you're a bespoke house-builder. You are unlikely to build multiple houses for the same customer. Unless, of course, you choose your customers right and work for the ultra-wealthy or developers only.

The marketplace is filled with offers, which are followed by a little more discount, then a little more, and a little more.

This trains your prospects and customers to wait, because they know a better deal will come by soon.

You should use your client-acquisition system to reverse this trend for your own business.

## Urgency and reward

Many of my clients implement a twelve-week conversion system.

Here is how it works for SSC.

The guys at SSC know that once they get to measure a customer's windows, they have a high conversion rate. For them, it's all about getting to the measure.

The focus of their twelve-week conversion system is to get you to take action and start moving towards having your windows measured.

As mentioned before, they generate around five or six hundred leads a month. These are usually people requesting a brochure by email or post. Once you do this, you fall into the twelve-week conversion system. The system has three stages, each lasting four weeks.

From weeks 1 to 4, you are offered a discount voucher of, say, 20%. As soon as you request the voucher code, the team gets in touch and take it from there. Should you not request the voucher code, you move to stage two.

From weeks 5 to 8, the system doesn't try to sell you anything and doesn't make you an offer. You are simply given more information about SSC and their product, such as testimonials and case studies from happy customers. There is no selling in this stage.

From weeks 9 to 12 (stage three), you are offered another discount voucher, but this time it is worth only 15%. This creates a feeling of having missed out and develops a sense of urgency, because you don't want to miss out again. It is made clear that the offer is only available for four weeks. (With an average order value of £2,500, the loss of 5% does make a difference.)

At the end of the twelve-week conversion system, you are removed from all sales sequences for ninety days, at which point you start all over again. The trick here is to apply the deadline not to making a purchase but to requesting the voucher code. SSC simply requests a show of intent and then takes it from there. This again allows the team to focus on those prospects who are nearest to being ready to buy.

Now you can run the numbers. SSC generates 500 leads a month and feeds them into their twelve-week conversion system. This means that after just six months they have 3,000 prospects somewhere in this process. The impact on the business has been nothing short of life-changing.

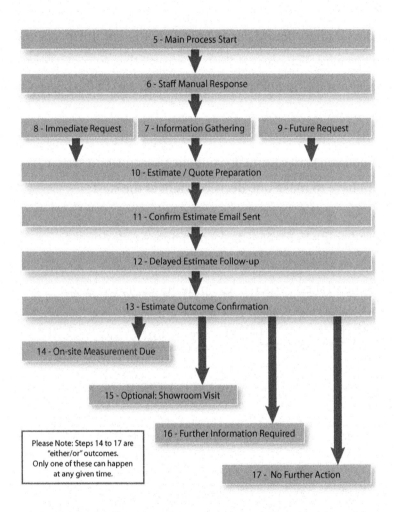

And this only works because it is a **system** – a system that never stops.

## Getting the work done

Your client-acquisition system can do more than run the offers and outbound communication to your prospects and customers. You also set it up to ensure that your employees carry out the manual tasks that make up part of the prospect-to-customer journey.

When you start setting up your client-acquisition system, you will have to make one decision right at the start:

Am I going to manage tasks or manage milestones?

As mentioned earlier, SSC's milestones are as follows:

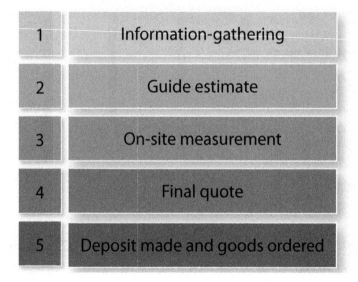

| 1 | Information-gathering |
| 2 | Guide estimate |
| 3 | On-site measurement |
| 4 | Final quote |
| 5 | Deposit made and goods ordered |

SSC decided to manage the individual tasks that lead to these milestones.

Which route is best for your business depends entirely on what you do and how your team works.

If you're running a sales team whose job it is to make lots of outbound calls and track the status of each prospect, you probably need only track milestones, not individual tasks. As such, you should not look to manage how many calls are made to every prospect, what is said, or when they call again. The investor membership example we've been using up to now is a good example. Their sales cycle can be two years long. As such, their sales process is relational, rather than functional.

If, on the other hand, you run a team whose job involves specific tasks, such as collecting information or sending out contracts, you will probably want to manage these tasks. This is especially useful when some team members depend on others to complete certain tasks before they can perform their own tasks.

Let's look at the SSC system in more detail, so you can see this in action. Here, we will only look at a section of their process to give you an idea of what they do. You can find more details at www.barefootbusinessthebook.com.

The steps we are looking at here (5 to 17) are shown in the following flow chart. Don't worry about what software is used for this – we'll look at that later.

**Step 5**. This is the handover from the lead-generation system to the client-acquisition system.

**Step 6**. A task is created for the first manual follow-up email or call.

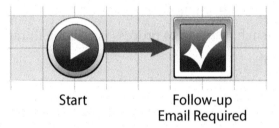

Start            Follow-up
                 Email Required

**Step 7**. The next task is to confirm that all the required information has been gathered.

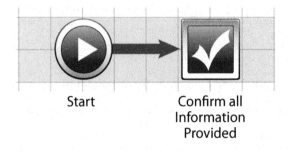

Start            Confirm all
                 Information
                 Provided

**Step 8.** Any customers who have additional requests straight after an installation are added to the main process so their requests can be dealt with in the same way as a new enquiry.

**Step 9.** After an installation, any customers who may have additional requests in the future are added to the main process, delayed until a specify date, so any additional requests can be dealt with in the same fashion as a new enquiry.

**Step 10.** A task is created to complete and compile all documents needed to process an estimate.

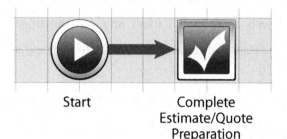

Start          Complete
Estimate/Quote
Preparation

**Step 11.** A task is created to confirm that the estimate has been sent out by email.

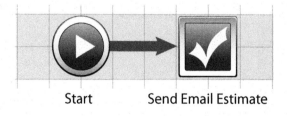

Start          Send Email Estimate

**Step 12.** The moment the estimate is confirmed as sent, a task is created to confirm the outcome.

Two days later, a first automated follow-up email is sent to the prospect. Six days after this, another automated follow-up email is sent to the customer. At this point, a task is also created to send out a post-estimate postcard.

Start | Complete Estimate Outcome Confirmation | Wait at least 2 days and then run on a weekday at 8.00am | First Follow-up | Wait at least 6 days and then run on a weekday at 8.00am | Second Follow-up | Send Post-Estimate Postcard

**Step 13.** Completing the "confirm estimate outcome" internal web form will cancel any outstanding estimate follow-up actions and pass the contact to the next step.

**Step 14.** When an estimate is confirmed as accepted, the four tasks shown below are created. The first of these is to arrange an on-site measurement.

Start | Book On-site Measurement | Compile Something Sweet | Assign Measure in Diary | Process Posting and Log

**Step 15.** If the estimate outcome is that the prospect needs to visit the showroom, this task will be created once the internal web form has been submitted.

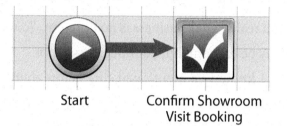

Start                Confirm Showroom
                        Visit Booking

**Step 16.** If the estimate outcome is that the prospect needs more information, a task will be created to confirm that this has been supplied.

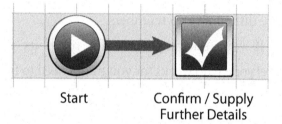

Start              Confirm / Supply
                      Further Details

**Step 17.** If the prospect does not want to go ahead with the purchase, they are marked "no further action". They will stay in the 52-week river and receive general marketing campaigns. The 52-week river consists of pre-written, fully automated email campaigns that aim to follow up with people over the long term. Remember, just because you are ready to sell it doesn't mean the prospect is ready to buy.

I must caution you against a few thoughts you might be having at this stage:

1 **My business is different.** It is extremely important that you realise your business is no different. Your product may be different but your business is not.

   I know I've mentioned this before, but I cannot stress this enough. You will sabotage your progress if you don't fully embrace this principle.

2 **My staff would never work like that.** Who owns your business? You are the one who set up the business and are taking all the risk. Yes, you need a team, but if they will not perform to your requirements, you need to hire different team members.

   If your business does not reach its potential, everyone who works for you might need to find a new job. Make this clear to your team.

3 **It will take a lot of work to work out and plan all this detail.**
   I cannot deny that you will need to put some regular, focussed effort into creating and then improving your systems, but the benefit far outweighs any effort you might have to put in. You don't need to start with a high level of detail. You can begin with the main milestones and slot further detail in as required.

## Fix the holes in the bucket

The reason this type of project management is so powerful for your business is that you can reach a stage where (almost) nobody falls through the cracks. You will be spending time and money on getting people into and through your lead-generation system.

If you don't have a solid client-acquisition system in place, you'll waste a lot of effort if you don't look after your prospects in a consistent and predictable way.

At first, you might feel as if you're restricting your staff's ability to do their jobs and let their personality shine through. But unless you run a theatre group, this is an important part of the system's function!

Ideally, you should be able to take anybody off the street and slot them into your team. They should know in as little time as possible what is expected of them and how to use the system that runs your business.

Few business can afford to let employees do things their own way.

CHAPTER FIVE

# Your Client Fulfilment System

Now that we've looked at the systems that get prospects through your door and buying from you, you might think the job is done. That's a big mistake.

The moment when a customer signs a contract or hands over money is the **most critical time**. And this is rightly so.

Your responsibility is to make sure you and your team have everything in place to make sure no balls are dropped.

Too many small businesses, and some of the big ones, forget the focus and structure required for great service delivery. Leaving the delivery of your product or service to chance, or allowing it to depend on the mood of a member of staff, can do more harm to your business than all the marketing in the world can fix.

This is why your client-fulfilment system should be as robust as your lead-generation and client-acquisition systems.

Consider the car industry again. I love Audi, and I've only bought Audis for years.

Their marketing is brilliant. They have angles to target all their demographic groups. The salespeople I've dealt with have always been professional and attentive. They make it easy to spend more money than you wanted to or thought you would, and you don't feel ripped off.

But none of that would matter if Audi couldn't deliver the cars. If the car was delivered late or I had to sort out niggles after it arrived, I don't think I'd have bought more than one.

I'd look at their advertising and their sales process with a bitter taste in my mouth, and this would make any further sales to me or my family difficult, if not impossible.

But because their client-fulfilment system is so good, I'm now on my fourth Audi in eight years. I don't think I would consider another car. Well, perhaps a Maserati or an Aston Martin, but they aren't as good for the school run! Mercedes or BMW simply don't have a chance with my family.

Now, I know you might be thinking, "I own a small business. I'm not competing with Audi."

Wrong. They *are* your competition.

You might not sell the same product, but you probably share customers. Audi, not just your direct competitors, are setting expectations in your customer's mind.

Amazon is a great example of this. My local bookstore has to meet the expectations set by Amazon. So does my local hi-fi store, and so does your business. Amazon sets the bar for service and delivery and the rest of us need to make sure we don't disappoint.

What expectations do your customers have, and are you meeting them? Are you and your team so good that you are setting expectations in your customer's mind?

Let's look at this from a specific example of a small business. We'll use SSC again and look at parts of their client-fulfilment system.

Their client-fulfilment system starts the moment a prospect accepts the quote and contract. This is when the prospect becomes a customer.

The operations side of the business does not know a project exists until the deposit is paid.

Why? Because there is no value in potential work taking up time and space in the operations department. The operations team can't do anything about it or affect the chances of getting the work. They focus entirely on serving customers, not prospects.

The first step in the SSC client-fulfilment system is to confirm the payment method and to confirm that the deposit has been paid. This is the trigger for everything else in the business to kick into action and for the operations team to take the project on board.

Once the deposit has been received, a welcome email and a letter in the post go out.

This confirms in detail what the next steps are and how the installation process will flow from here, making sure that the customer knows what to expect.

At this point, the process splits into two parallel streams: admin and operations.

The operations team get on with the detail of the design and ordering from the factory, while the admin team makes sure everything is confirmed with the finance department and so on.

The moment the order is placed with the factory, the customer is automatically notified. They never feel left in the dark.

Keeping the customer updated is extremely important for SSC, because there is a long time-lag between order and installation.

All their installations are designed in-house and made in China. This means that from the moment you pay your deposit, you will wait at least ten weeks before your installation. All you can do is wait: there is nothing they can do to speed this up or keep you entertained in the meantime. Or is there?

A couple of weeks after placing your order, you receive an automated email to tell you the estimated delivery date, based on the ship's estimated docking date.

This is simply a friendly reminder that you've not been forgotten now you've handed over your money.

Then on week 5, you receive a postcard in the mail. The postcard shows a ship filled with containers, all with the SSC logo emblazoned on them.

This is basically a postcard from your shutters, telling you they are on the way, somewhere on the high seas.

While these little touch points may seem trivial, the impact is real. The goodwill it builds in the relationship with the customer can't be bought or faked.

Two weeks before the proposed installation date – a date that was set more than two months ago, remember – you receive a call from the office to confirm the date is still suitable.

One week before the installation date an email goes out, which details the installation process and what to expect… right down to the detail of who will remove the rubbish and packaging.

You can see that this system gives the guys at SSC a lot to do. It would be so much easier to just take the deposit and forget about the customer for the next ten weeks, which is what many small businesses do. But then most small businesses don't enjoy the growth and financial success of companies like SSC, because they don't have systems.

## How do I keep track of all this?

The answer is systems and automation.

You could employ someone full-time (£15,000–£22,000 a year) to keep track of who is where on the journey. You could use a spreadsheet and manually update the information for every customer every morning. But I bet things would be forgotten and people would fall through the cracks.

Your other option is to invest in having a system designed and built. You don't need to have a bespoke piece of software built. You can have your system built inside a piece of software that starts from £7.20 per month and maxes out around £280 per month, depending on your needs.

A system allows your entire business to operate like a production line, and production lines are predictable and have real value. Hoping that John remembers to do something has no value to you or the business. It's far better to tell John what to do every morning, without it taking up any of your time.

## Generating repeat business, automatically

Many small-business owners think about the first sale only. If that's all they focus on, it means they're always chasing new clients, and, in the process, forgetting about or neglecting existing ones.

A simple example is the window cleaner who works in my local area. We belonged to the same business mentoring group many years ago.

Every now and then, he knocks on my door to see if I want the windows cleaned. And when I say every now and then, I mean once every eighteen months!

The last time he knocked on the door I let him clean the windows again. I told him, directly, that if he came by every three months instead of every eighteen months, I would happily have him clean the windows. I am never going to ring a window cleaner: I don't care enough. But if he shows up, the work is his.

Simply having a system in place that emails me every three months to see if I want him to clean the windows and reminds him every three months to come round to my house would mean that I pay him six times in eighteen months, not once. If he rolled this out to all his customers, he would more than double his business overnight, without the need to find a single new customer.

Are you making the same mistake? How are you making sure you get as much business as possible from your existing customers?

You are letting your customers down if you don't have automatic follow-up and reminders of "service required" as part of your system.

If the window cleaner came round every three months, I would happily recommend him to my neighbours and anyone else I know in the area. Once every eighteen months is bad service, especially for a service that needs repeating or a product that needs replacing.

Some of you might be thinking, "But my product is expensive and lasts for years. I can't do this."

Really? How is Audi able to sell my family four cars in eight years, then? It's simple: they changed their business model.

At no point do they say that the car I am buying will last for twenty years. They simply get me on a three-year finance deal with a balloon payment at the end.

This balloon payment is a good earner for them, but few car owners actually make the payment.

The last time we upgraded to a newer car, everything was set up from the get-go to ensure we took another car at the end of the three years instead of paying fully for the one we'd just ordered.

The conversation went along the lines of:

"At the end of three years, you can either give us several thousand pounds and keep this car, or you can keep making payments to us and come and pick up a brand new car.

When it came to it, guess what the extra cost was for a brand new car? An additional £10 million!"

This is the power of having a client-fulfilment system that knows your customers and makes sales for you.

We didn't even know the car was at the end of the finance agreement. We weren't looking for a new car, and we had no intention of getting one. That is, until we received a letter from our Audi garage making us the offer. All of a sudden, we wanted a new car.

That's the magic of systems.

The other excellent part of Audi's client-fulfilment system is the aftercare element.

They understand that their relationship with you does not end the moment they sell you a car. That's just the start.

I don't need to remember when to service or MOT the car, because Audi let me know. This also ensures I become a little lazy. I have no interest in going out and finding a garage that can service the car. When they write me a letter, I call them and book it in. It's simple and easy for me, and it's highly profitable for them.

Don't assume this is just for the big companies. If my local garage, which is a two-minute walk from me, was to put lead-generation, client-acquisition and client-fulfilment systems in place, they might well get and keep my MOT and servicing business. Without these systems, there's no chance.

Your business needs an element of aftercare in your client-fulfilment system.

Even an email to say "I hope you are still enjoying X", sent automatically to every customer six months after their last transaction, can generate extra income for your business.

SSC generate a lot of their income in this way. Let's say someone had shutters installed in their kitchen six months ago, and now they receive an offer by email. They are reminded of the great service and product that SSC provided. They've been thinking about getting some shutters for the master bedroom and the lounge, and the offer is just enough to tip them over the edge; they place the order that week.

Without the email they might still have ordered the shutters, but would they have ordered them from SSC? Would they remember to do business with SSC?

Imagine you sell kitchens. Now, most kitchen installers I've met (and I used to be one myself) think you can only sell someone a kitchen once every ten years or so. There's no real repeat business here, right?

Wrong! What if you set your system up in the following way?

You offer customers a free service check for their new kitchen at the following intervals:

- One year after installation
- Two years after installation
- Three years after installation
- Five years after installation.

You go round for a couple of hours to make sure all the hinges are set correctly, and so on.

This will benefit your business in two main ways:

1 When you send the customer the email about the service check in year 3, you might find out that they're about to move house. Suddenly, there's potential for a conversation about a new kitchen installation that you might otherwise have missed out on.

2  Because the customer loves the regular service check so much, they recommend you to everyone they speak to.

By setting this up using an automated system that communicates with every one of your customers, you will be in a position to grow your business and create repeat business without constantly chasing new clients. The clients will come to you.

With decent lead-generation, client-acquisition and client-fulfilment systems in place, you'll create a business you won't recognise – in a good way!

You'll stop feeling like a madman, having to do everything yourself – even at midnight. Instead, you'll realise you've built a real business. A business of value, which gives your customers a brilliant service. A business that gives you the life you dreamed of when you first started out. A business that doesn't need you any more but provides for you and your loved ones.

By now, I hope you have a good grasp of why you should have systems in your business.

In the next section, we'll look at the 'How' and the 'What'. So, fasten your seat belts...

# CHAPTER SIX

# How Do I Do This?

So far, I've done my best to show you why there are only three key systems in any business and why they should be in place in **your** business.

All your other systems form part of these three systems, performing specific functions within one or all of them.

And when you're thinking of the tools (software or otherwise) to build your systems, please think holistically. **Everything** relates back to these three systems, and everything should be in service of the three key systems.

Now, I can hear the voice in your head saying "OK, I get it. This is all brilliant. I want these systems. But how and where on earth do I start?"

## White-room process (day one)

Everything starts with your white-room process.

A true white-room process is exactly what it sounds like. (Photography studios work really well for this.)

You and the members of your team lock yourselves away, ideally for forty-eight hours, in a white room.

- No phones
- No email
- No interruptions

The aim of your forty-eight-hour lockdown is to redesign your business. You are going to focus all your energy on designing the ideal customer journey.

Did you ever **design** your business in the first place? If you're like most business owners I speak to, I suspect it just ended up the way it is rather than being planned that way.

Seldom do I come across a business that's had any design go into the systems or processes. Most businesses are run on the premise of "this is the way I was shown".

And here's the challenge with that.

There was once a disturbing and thought-provoking science experiment, which went something like this:

> Three monkeys were locked in a cage, with a ladder in the middle.
>
> From time to time, some food would appear at the top of the ladder.
>
> Whenever a monkey was half-way up the ladder, the monkeys on the floor would get an electric shock.
>
> The monkeys soon caught on to what triggered the electric shock. This made them attack any monkey who looked as if they were going to climb the ladder.
>
> After some time, the electric shock was removed from the experiment, but the monkeys still attacked any monkey who tried to climb the ladder.
>
> The monkeys were replaced, one at a time, several times.
>
> After the entire group had been replaced three times, the behaviour still persisted, even though none of the monkeys in the cage had ever experienced the electric shock.
>
> They had simply learned the behaviour "this is how we do things here".

And this is how most businesses are run. Seldom does anyone stop and ask "Why do we do it this way?"

This is the magic of the white-room process.

You get to review your entire business: every function, every step, every role.

Imagine your living room. Did you buy every piece of furniture with purpose? Did it just end up that way because that's the furniture you had when you moved from your last property?

Now imagine you take everything out of the room. You paint the room completely white before you start planning how to decorate and furnish it. Would you still put your old furniture in the room? What would you put in the room if you started from scratch?

It is vitally important to focus on your business in this way when you go through your white-room process. Don't let yourself off the hook.

Don't keep anything unless it drives the business you want.

This is not an exercise in making what you have slightly better. This is about real transformation for you and your business.

I cannot stress this enough. You're not just trying to improve what you already have and what you already do. Your aim is to create your business as if it is day one, but you get to keep all your and your team's experience.

**Involve team members and outsiders**
When doing your white-room process, it is vital to involve people from all parts of your business. Don't just get in the room with the managers or high-level team members. Get input from team members on all levels. Don't try to second-guess what the operations team need or what the front-of-house team really experience. They are the ones who speak to your customers and suppliers the most. In some ways, they know your business better than you do.

If you have a small team, get the whole team involved. Make it clear at the outset that nothing is sacred and all suggestions will be heard.

The white room should be an environment where everyone can be challenged, no matter what their position in the business. If you're concerned about how your team might respond to this, you might want to get an external person involved to facilitate the discussion.

Getting an external person to lead the discussion can also be an extremely effective way to ensure everyone in the team gives their input. This helps to make sure that less senior members of your team feel that they can speak up, but also ensures more senior members take everyone's input onboard.

For example, I once led a white-room process for a large cruise-holiday provider.

I had never been on a cruise, and I knew nothing about the business.

We were discussing the different brands they offered, when my client had a moment of insight that they would not have had without external input.

Two of the brands that came up were Norwegian Cruise Lines and Royal Caribbean.

Now, I made a statement based on my assumption that Royal Caribbean goes to the Caribbean and Norwegian Cruise Lines goes around the Norwegian Fjords.

And although I know now that this is not the case at all, my mistaken belief made them realise it was wrong to assume their prospects knew that both cruise lines go all over the world.

Sometimes, ignorance is exactly what you need in the room.

## The duck on a lake

The second crucial point to focus on throughout this whole process is that every step should initially be designed from the customer's perspective.

Don't fall into the trap of looking at what is easiest for the staff or what is cheapest or quickest. Put all your focus on the customer and then work out how to achieve **that**.

Think of a duck gliding across a lake on a crisp autumn morning. The lake is as flat as a mirror, save for a gracefully gliding duck. People flock to take photos to post on Facebook, use in a calendar and so on.

Nobody ever tries to take pictures of the duck's feet frantically kicking about under the water. Nobody cares about the duck's feet.

The success of your white-room process depends on making a clear distinction between your customer's experience (the duck) and the internal workings and processes of your business (the feet underwater).

Take Amazon, for example.

As an author, I drool over Amazon's processes and systems for warehouse management, stock allocation and dispatch. You could give me a week-long tour and I'm sure I'd still want more by the end of it.

As a reader, ordering a book to be delivered before 5pm on Monday, I don't care about Amazon's systems at all. I only care about the outcome of those wonderfully complex systems – my book arriving the next day.

Again, you might not sell books online, but Amazon sets and confirms your customers' expectations with every order, long before they buy from you. How do you compare?

**If this, then that**

Start the design of your ideal customer journey with a straight-line process. You can add the contingencies later.

The straight-line process shown below shows what happens in a business-like SSC. This is a simplified form of what really happens.

Here, you can see a simple process from **enquiry** to **estimate** to **measurement** to **quote** to **order** to **installation.**

This is the basic customer journey in their business.

The problem is that customers are human beings who do their own thing, and you need to accommodate that. **The key is that every contingency you build into the system drives the prospect back to one of your straight-line milestones.**

Every prospect and customer will experience and hit these milestones, but they are free to do so at their own pace.

Compare a journey on the London Underground with a journey on the bus.

The London Underground is your milestone journey. You get on at particular points and get off at particular points. You can't get on or off between destinations. If you travel from Leicester Square to Green Park, you can't stop off to have a look at Piccadilly Circus or Fortnum & Mason. The journey is rigid.

If you were to walk or travel by taxi it's completely different.

If you want to go from Leicester Square to Green Park, you can go via Trafalgar Square or Oxford Street. Stop off on Haymarket and have a look around Piccadilly Circus. You can ask the taxi driver to wait outside Waterstones while you find a book to read in the park, get back in the taxi and head for Fortnum & Mason for afternoon tea, and finally walk down to Green Park.

And that's your ideal customer journey. They need to reach rigid milestones to do business with you, but there is near complete flexibility in how they reach those milestones.

The flow-chart below shows an updated version of the SSC milestone journey, with the contingencies built in.

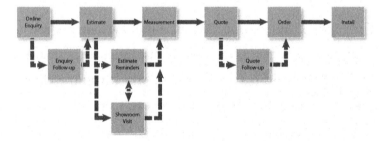

**How to do your white-room process**

**Step 1: Don't plan anything. Don't give people homework.**

When I lead a white-room process for clients, I am always asked "Do you want us to prepare anything, bring anything with us?"

My answer is always "Don't prepare anything. Just bring the knowledge you already have of your business and the members of your team you want in the room."

The whole purpose is to start with a blank slate. Don't turn up with preconceived ideas or outcomes. Have a clear mind and leave your old ideas at the door.

**Step 2: Make sure you have plenty of magic whiteboard.**

You could use normal whiteboards, but they are fixed and you don't want to be in a situation where you have to rub off what you wrote in the morning to be able to continue after lunch.

You'll want to use plenty of different colours, too.

Use one colour for the milestone journey, another for the different contingencies, and different colours for the internal process and details.

**Step 3: Start with the customer journey.**

Start by mapping out the ideal customer journey in the top half of your whiteboards. You'll want to structure this with an eye on the three key systems discussed in this book. There's no need to be too fixed at this stage – just keep them in mind.

Draw out, step by step, what you want your customer to experience on the ideal journey.

Pay attention to all points of communication, marketing, updates, progress reports and so on.

Don't get drawn into conversations about how you'll do this. There will be people in the room – and one of them might be you – who will want to know how it will all be done. Now is not the time for that: you're in the design stage.

**Step 4: Look at the internal process.**

Now focus on what needs to happen in the business to make sure every customer experiences the journey you designed in Step 3.

Again, the trick here is not to focus on tools. You are not concerned with the **how** yet, only with the **what**.

You can view the diagram that shows this process for SSC at www.barefootbusinessthebook.com

You will see there is no mention of any specific tool or piece of software. There are merely actions to be performed.

Think of it as hanging a picture on the wall.

The customer journey is the picture. The internal process is the hole in the wall with a hook for the picture to hang on.

In the next chapter we will look at the details of how to drill the hole. Is it a plasterboard or brick wall? Do I need a hammer drill or will a driver work? Do I need one hook or two?

All of these technical questions are for the second phase of your white-room process, and doing the research will take you outside your white-room process.

Once you have gone through this process for the entire customer journey (from lead, to prospect, to customer, to repeat purchase) and what needs to happen in the business, you should be at the end of your first day.

It's important to focus on getting this done in one day. Don't turn it into a week-long exercise: you will waste time and lose focus.

Work fast. Make a start, then improve.

## White-room process (day two)

You're now going to go back over the whole journey you've mapped out, from start to finish.

Here, the discussion should focus on three points.

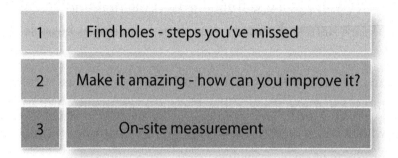

| 1 | Find holes - steps you've missed |
| 2 | Make it amazing - how can you improve it? |
| 3 | On-site measurement |

Spend your second day making sure you've not missed out anything fundamental to your business – perhaps things that you and your team just take for granted. Slot them into the drawings where you can, or add them on extra sheets as detailed outlines.

Look at how to create an amazing experience for your customers.

Brainstorm crazy ideas which, until now, the functional side of your discussion has not allowed for. Again, don't consider the how – just dig into the what.

This is where ideas like the box of treats for the customer's dog and the postcard of a shipping container come from. Explore. Don't dismiss any suggestions outright. Note down the craziest ones and explore the ones that spark conversation.

**What to consider**

**Don't worry about getting it perfect the first time round.**
Make a start, and get to version three as quickly as possible.

You'll find that once you start looking at your business in this much detail, you'll never stop. It becomes an ongoing process, which will change and develop as your team grows and your products or services evolve.

It will never be perfect and you will never finish it.

With that in mind, the most important thing is for you to start.

**Just start**

Once you do, you will find you uncover things you had never thought of before.

The isolation of the white-room process lets you focus on your business for an intense extended period, but it means nothing if you don't test the outcome on your customers.

You need to expect and embrace a little bit of chaos. Things will go wrong and you will need to apologise from time to time, but the rewards are huge.

The key here is to take action. You can sit around thinking about the finer details of this for the next 10 years and still not achieve anything, but by starting you will make progress and also uncover opportunities for improvement you could never reach by just thinking.

**Your team**

The white-room process is designed to let team members buy into the process and become part of what shapes the business. This has an unbelievably positive effect on teams.

You will find some bright stars you didn't realise you had. What's more, they will have an ongoing input into the future of the system – and your business. To them, this will no longer be just a job.

Now that we've done the fun design bits, let's get into the real technical bit. What do you use for what, and where do you use it?

# CHAPTER SEVEN

# What Tools Do I Use?

Now that you have a clearly designed ideal customer journey, how do you make it a reality?

How do you turn it into a complete system that sits at the heart of your business?

We'll break everything down into your business' three key systems. We'll deal with everything under those three headings.

Because things change so rapidly in the worlds of technology and business, the information on the specific tools and software included in this book will become out of date.

That's why you can always go to www.barefootfusiness thebook.com to view up-to-date information on any of the technical and software-specific information mentioned in this chapter.

## Lead-generation system

When it comes to lead generation, most small-business owners fall into one of two groups.

1  **Those who hold onto the past for dear life.** They will only advertise in the papers and magazines they've always used. They're happy to waste money on *Thompson Local* or the *Yellow Pages*. They don't know if the marketing is working or not, but they won't change what they're doing or try anything new in case it doesn't work.

2  **Those who try everything new at least once.** They'll run after every new shiny opportunity like a magpie chasing a bit of silver foil blowing in the wind. What they have in common with the first group is they aren't too sure if their marketing is working either. They never stick with one form of marketing for long enough to master it or see any returns.

The underlying issue for both groups is the same. They don't know what, if anything, works.

Your lead-generation system relies fully on you knowing your ideal customer better than anyone else does. I'm not talking about the big questions: whether they're male or female, where they live, or how old they are.

Go deeper than that.

What car do they drive? Where were they educated? What books do they read? How many kids do they have? You can find a more complete list to help you create your ideal customer avatar at www.barefootbusinessthebook.com.

The key here is to follow the following steps, in this order:

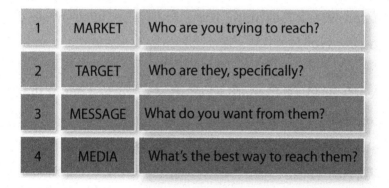

| 1 | MARKET | Who are you trying to reach? |
|---|--------|------------------------------|
| 2 | TARGET | Who are they, specifically? |
| 3 | MESSAGE | What do you want from them? |
| 4 | MEDIA | What's the best way to reach them? |

It is vital to follow these steps in order. Too many business owners see a new marketing tool, or stick to their favourite media, and then try to work out how to use it – without thinking about whether it's suitable for communicating with the people they want to reach.

Let's look at one type of media: flyers.

Do you think dropping flyers around the neighbourhood would be a good form of marketing?

That depends on what your business is and who you want to reach.

If you run the local gardening service or MOT garage, this could be an extremely effective form of marketing.

If you were a locksmith, it would be a complete waste of money. Why?

People need a locksmith when they are locked out of their house. Do they know when they'll be locked out? No. Does anybody want what you are selling? Most of the time, no. But on the few occasions they do, they want it so much you can charge what you like. The problem with dropping flyers advertising a locksmith is that even if someone keeps the flyer on the fridge for the next six months, it will still be on the fridge when they're locked out of the house. It will be completely useless to them as they stand outside their front door in the rain. And it'll be useless to the locksmith, too.

The one place you really want to be as a locksmith is on Google Search. Why?

Because as your prospect is standing outside their front door, trying the key for the forty-seventh time just in case it works, they'll be searching on their smartphone for "local locksmith" or "emergency locksmith" and you want to be there. And that's what Google Search does for you.

Let's look at some specific examples and go through the four steps: market, target, message, media. We'll ask the important questions when working out how to get people into a lead-generation system. Who am I looking for? What "state" are they in when they're looking for me or my service?

## Market

At one level, my market is the five million small-business owners in the UK. But how could I possibly craft a marketing message that would resonate with all these small-business owners?

What could I possibly write in my advert or article that would resonate with a specialist aluminium manufacturer, the local printer and the village coffee shop? I can't.

When you are looking at communicating with your market, you need to zone in and focus each campaign on a specific target.

## Target

Because there is no way I could successfully communicate with all the five million business owners in the market, I have chosen a specific target within that market.

My target market is as follows:

**LOCAL BUSINESSES**
I can carry out targeted campaigns to reach
this section of the market.

**BUSINESSES WITH BETWEEN TWO AND TEN EMPLOYEES**
They need systems and support.
They have a real business and take it seriously.

**BUSINESSES WITH A TURNOVER OF £500,000 OR MORE**
They are more likely to be able to afford our service.

**BUSINESSES WITH AN AVERAGE TRANSACTION VALUE
OF AT LEAST £2,000**
Generating a small number of extra sales
can have a real impact on these businesses.

**BUSINESSES IN THE HOME-MAKER SECTOR**
(blinds, shutters, kitchens, bathrooms and so on).
My team has over forty years' combined experience in this market.

**BUSINESS OWNERS AGED BETWEEN 30 AND 55**
They are still hungry and willing to make changes to their business.

You can see we are very specific with our target. And so should you be.

I know what you might be thinking: "What about a business that has fifteen employees and the owner is 60?"

We would still be happy to talk to them and work together, if they came to us. But we don't design any of our marketing to target that sector.

In choosing your target, you are not actively turning business away. You are just choosing to focus on the business you really want and the people you can help the most.

**Message**
Now that you've defined your target within your market, crafting your message will be much easier.

Let's look at an example from Audi.

Audi ran a TV advert in the UK in for the R8 V10 Plus. The ad shows the car in a test tunnel. It's sitting on those rollers that let you drive as fast as possible without actually going anywhere.

All they do in the ad is start the engine, show us a little bit of the car, and go through all the gears up to top speed – with close-up shots of the engine and the fire spitting out of the exhaust.

This message is crafted to sell the R8 to men who like super-cars, love the sound of the roaring engines and want to show off a bit when driving down the high street. This ad speaks directly to that person. They aren't trying to sell that car to my mother. If they wanted to do that, they'd talk about comfort and safety.

Can you see how knowing exactly who you're trying to speak to completely transforms the message you put out there?

To be clear, you can have multiple ideal customer avatars for your business, but you need to define them and keep them separate.

For instance, if you were running an interiors business and you offered kitchens, bathrooms, bedrooms and small building works, you need to keep these as distinct audiences.

If I am in the market for a new bathroom fit out, I will have little interest in your kitchen worktops article or mailer. Speak to me about what I am interested in at the time.

Clearly, once you have my attention and I am part of your client-acquisition system, then you can tell me about all the other services you offer, but with the first message you need to appear to be exactly the right place for me.

For my business, the message is clear: "How would you like to start generating 500 leads a month for your local business, double your business, and be able to take more time off?"

For your marketing messages to be as effective as possible, you need to define your target audience as an individual, and then write for that person specifically.

In defining your customer avatar, you can start by asking the following questions:

- Is my idea customer male or female?
- Are they under- or over-45?
- What car do they drive?
- Where do they shop?
- What are their favourite magazines or newspapers?

- Who are their favourite authors?
- How much do they earn?

You need to really get into their way of life and what is important to them. You can find a more complete list and article on how to define your ideal customer avatar at www.barefootbusinessthebook.com

## Media

The Audi R8 advert mentioned above would be shown on TV during breaks on shows like *Top Gear*, sports programmes and action films. They know who the customer is, what the message is and when and how to reach them.

Google Search is an immensely powerful marketing tool, but it would be useless if Audi banked on it to sell the R8. Nobody would ever go and search for it.

Once someone has seen the advert on TV, they might visit the Audi website to learn more (at this point, Google Display Remarketing would become useful). Only then might they use Google Search to find their local Audi dealer.

Can you see how the same media can be brilliant or useless, depending on what you want to achieve? A hammer is the perfect tool for banging nails into the wall to hang pictures, but it's useless for painting those same walls. Not because hammers are useless; they just aren't made for painting walls.

Let's look at some different media.

■ **Google Search**

These are the ads you see when you search for something in Google, shown below.

**Locksmith in Surrey - Your Local Locksmith Specialist**
**Ad** www.southernlockandsafe.co.uk/ ▼
Contact Us For More Information.
Product guarantees · Great customer service · Fast delivery · Free delivery

In simple terms, you tell Google what **search terms** (the words that people type into the search box) you want your advert to appear for. It works like an auction, so you also tell Google how much you are willing to pay every time someone clicks on your ad.

You can be extremely targeted with this. When done properly it can become complex, but if it will reach your target market it is well worth it. A word of caution, though – it is easy to pay what has become known as the Google Stupidity Tax. For some time, when people ran a search for "baby" an ad would appear for eBay, telling you that you can buy a baby, lowest prices guaranteed! This was due to someone at eBay not setting up their keyword-matching correctly in the Google Ad creator.

■ **Google Display**

There are two main functions to Google Display: remarketing and placements.

**Remarketing** is when you go and look for something on a website and then, when you go to a different website, you see ads for the thing you were just looking at. This is not just for big businesses – you can do it too!

**Placements** are when you tell Google where you want your ads to show, without waiting for someone to come to your website first. For example, if you were running a local tanning salon, you could tell Google to place your ads on the *Cosmopolitan* website, but only for people who live within three miles of your salon. This is very targeted display advertising.

### ▪ Facebook advertising

Yes, your customers are on Facebook. And Facebook advertising is not about getting "likes"; it's about generating new business, with a direct call to action.

Facebook allows you to target a specific audience based on their behaviour and what they like or have an interest in, their work, their favourite sports and so on.

This means you can create ads, that are targeted specifically at the people you want to reach.

Like Google, Facebook has a remarketing function, which lets you market only to those people who have visited your website.

### ▪ Direct mail

Old-school snail mail can still be really effective for the right types of businesses. Google sends out direct mail – why don't you?

Like all media, the key to successful direct mail is that it is the right tool for the audience you want to reach. You also need to track everything, or you won't know if it works.

When you send out direct mail, make sure you have a separate web link for every marketing campaign, and use a different tracking number (virtual phone numbers) if you want people to call you. In this way, you can see exactly how many phone calls or website visits each piece of direct mail has produced, rather than relying on a gut feeling about whether or not a campaign is working.

### ▪ Bought lists

One thing small-business owners seem to be unaware of is that they can now play the same game as the big businesses. The playing field has been levelled far more than you might realise.

Let's say you want to reach professional women aged 30 to 45, who have two kids under five and who live in south-east England. You can buy that list, with postal addresses, and send prospects direct mail that drives them online and into your client-acquisition system.

What if you want to reach all the kitchen and bathroom installers in the UK? You can buy or rent this type of information so you can reach your target market direct. There is no need for you to run a blanket flyer campaign in the hope of reaching a few ideal clients. If you put in the time to identify your market properly, you can spend your marketing budget with a higher level of intelligence and effectiveness.

Can you see how and why targeting is so important when you're choosing what media to use?

## Client-acquisition system

For your business to function well with the three key systems in place, you must decide on some core tools.

These will cover three main areas:

1 Communication with prospects
2 Internal communication
3 Task and project management.

The key here is to choose the tools that work best for your business, and those that enable you to provide the ideal customer journey you designed during your white-room process.

## Communication with prospects

Here, you need to focus on having the right level of automation and flexibility. Choose tools that allow you to communicate with hundreds of ideal prospects in as personal but as automated a way as possible.

When your lead-generation system is working properly, you'll find that you generate more enquiries than you can possibly deal with by relying on notebooks and email. You'll need a system to record and display the history of your relationship with every prospect.

Automation also lets your system communicate with hundreds (if not thousands) of interested prospects, filtering them so your team can put their energy into the hot, ready-to-buy prospects.

As with most software platforms, there are many options to choose from and everyone has their favourites.

My personal favourites are Infusionsoft and Active Campaign.

Both share many of the same functions, including email automation, sales-pipeline management and basic task management. Infusionsoft also has an e-commerce element to it, allowing you to sell goods and services directly online, taking credit card payments online and integrating with stock-control and dispatch systems. There are many different plug-ins and add-ons for these software packages; not as many for Active Campaign yet, as this is the newer kid on the block. (For a detailed overview, visit www.barefootbusinessthebook.com.)

**How do you communicate with over five hundred leads a month?**

This is a question that comes up time and again. It's one of the things people think they won't be able to do when they begin using systems and automation.

The trick is in the planning. You need to be willing to do the hard work at this stage that will make the selling easy. At the same time, make sure the automated communications you send out provide real value to your prospects. If they read your emails, they should feel good about the value they have received from you even if they never buy from you.

**Ask your prospect what they want**

We implement a system inspired by Ryan Levesque's ask method.

We're going to get a bit technical here, so stay with me. (You can also follow the video walkthrough at www.barefoot businessthebook.com.)

There's a time and place for providing a link to a free guide to your product or service on your website. But at some point you and your prospects will benefit if they complete a well-designed questionnaire.

This is usually made up of twelve to twenty questions and it should give the prospect a tailor-made solution or diagnosis.

Each question has at least three answers to choose from, but the prospect can choose only one answer to each question. You should choose the questions and answer options carefully to perform two important functions.

1 Provide the prospect with useful and relevant feedback
2 Provide you with real insight into what your prospect actually wants.

Once the prospect completes the questionnaire, they receive a report followed by personalised feedback over a number of weeks.

This system allows you to create a custom report for every visitor to your website.

Let's look at this in more detail.

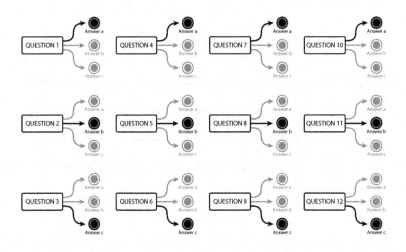

In the example above you can see twelve questions, with three answer options each. I've highlighted the answers chosen for our example.

This is where the magic starts to happen! You now have twelve points of data on this particular prospect. You can now use this information to determine what communication you send to this prospect over the next two or three weeks.

The following image shows you all the emails you could send, based on which answers the prospect gives. I've highlighted the ones you would need to send to our example prospect.

This means the prospect will receive the following email sequence:

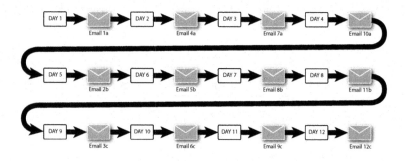

This does mean you have to write a lot of emails to put this type of system in place – but that's where its power lies. Make the effort to put your systems and processes in place to beat the competition.

The real power of your systems and processes, and this type of targeted communication with your prospects, is that your competition only ever sees the tip of the iceberg. They can see the tailored outcomes for the prospect but they can't see how the system works internally. They will never be able to reverse-engineer your system.

While you've done the hard work to create a unique universe and personal, first-impression experience for each of your prospects, your competition keeps churning out the same old "buy my stuff, 10% off" line, the same as everyone else.

**You can take this one step further**

Depending on the business you are in, you can use the above question-and-answer system to provide a diagnosis or score for your prospect, possibly with advice on how to improve.

For example, if you are in consulting or professional services, you could do the following.

Let's give each answer a **weighting** – that is, a number of points.

- Option A = 7 points
- Option B = 5 points
- Option C = 3 points.

In our example above, the prospect would get a total score of 60 out of a possible 92.

You could then create a tailored report email for your prospects, depending on their score within a range:

- Email 1: 0–20
- Email 2: 21–38
- Email 3: 39–56
- Email 4: 57–79
- Email 5: 80–92.

Can you see how this would allow you to speak to each group of customers based on their level of experience or the service level required?

**What should I sell?**

This type of system can also help you to decide what offer to initially place in front of each prospect.

Let's group the questions we used in our previous example into sections. Each section represents certain product options.

- Questions 1–4: Product A
- Questions 5–8: Product B
- Questions 9–12: Product C.

If you worked out a score for each section of the questionnaire, following our example, where A = 7 points, B = 5 points and C = 3 Points:

- Questions 1 – 4 Total = 22 points
- Questions 5 – 8 Total = 20 points
- Questions 9 – 12 Total = 18 points.

This tells you that the prospect's biggest need is for the product covered in section C (Questions 9 -12) as we are looking for the section with the lowest score, so that should be the first offer you place in front of them.

Make your communication so relevant and personal that your prospects feel as if they're the only person you're dealing with, and they'll travel through their own unique universe right to your door.

**Internal communication**
Don't use email for internal communication. It's outdated and not fit for the business you are trying to create.

The big flaw in using email for internal communication is that it is not collaborative.

I'll give you an example:

> My wife is a doctor in the NHS. She was part of a team of around twenty-five other doctors and nurses who work in the same department.
>
> Different doctors and nurses deal with the same patients over long periods of time, in different capacities. They share information by email to make sure everyone is up to speed.
>
> Because multiple doctors from multiple disciplines share responsibility for a patient's care, they need to make sure everyone is aware of every discussion. As they rely so heavily on email, this creates the situation where everyone copies in everyone else on every email!
>
> This leads to a situation where a highly qualified doctor can easily spend two hours at the end of the day sifting through emails, looking for the ones that might need input and action. Think about the efficiency savings that just this one department could make if they used different internal communication tools.

Another reason email is so flawed for internal communication is that it is not transparent. Here's an example:

> Let's say you have a team of ten people in your business.
>
> When John sent an email to ask Jane a question last Monday morning, nobody else knew about it. (Unless your team adopts the onerous practice of copying everyone in, as described above.) The thing is, Jane doesn't work on Mondays, so John had to wait until Tuesday for an answer. But Geoff could have quickly and easily answered John's question if he had known about it. This would have made your team more effective and productive.

A far better scenario would be if the whole team could see John's question. Anyone in the team could answer, and everyone else in the team would see the answer. This creates a situation where your team is essentially just having conversations. Everyone can get involved and share their knowledge "in the moment".

So, if email is so bad, what should you use instead?

Enter the software-development geeks. They solved this problem quite some time ago, and we are now catching on. There are many platforms to choose from, and the ideal customer journey you designed in your white-room process should help you decide which is most suitable.

My favourite tool for this is Slack.

Slack allows you to set up channels and invite members to these channels.

For example, you could have a management channel, a finance channel, a sales channel, an operations channel and a marketing channel.

Set up each channel so only the relevant team members have access to it. You can then have open discussions in the management channel, for example, knowing that only managers can take part in the conversation.

Essentially, Slack allows you to have a Facebook-style thread for each section of your business, without the distraction of the rest of Facebook.

If you run large projects, you can create a channel for each project and invite every team member who is working on that project. They can then contribute, without being inundated by conversations about projects they do not work on.

**Task and project management**
This is the part of your internal systems that will probably need the most research and trialling.

Every project-management package on the market approaches it from the angle of what the developers and their clients needed. Experiment to find the one that works best for you.

The two main packages are:

1 Packages based on checklists
2 Packages based on boards.

If you and your team often work from checklists, look for a platform that allows you to create tasks in that form. Wunderlist, Wrike and Teamwork are some good examples.

In the boards camp, you will find products like Trello and JIRA. Imagine every project has its own whiteboard, divided into columns for new tasks, tasks in progress, and tasks that have been done. Think of all your tasks as sticky notes. They start in the left-hand column for new tasks; as the tasks are worked on, you move the sticky notes across the board. That is the basis for these platforms, and it can be a great way to run projects.

## Integration

The main question we have to ask when deciding on what tools to use when building systems for our clients is: How well does it interact with the others?

The software packages you use have to integrate with each other.

Here's an example:

Let's say you and I are having a conversation in Slack. As a result of our conversation, I realise there are a couple of tasks for Dave to complete. The system is set up, so all I do is type:
@dave New Task Description #Task
This creates a task on the project's Trello board and

assigns it to Dave. Dave doesn't need to be in Slack for this to work. He can be working with the operations team or out on the road, but the task will appear for him and Trello will notify him.

I also need to know when Dave has done his bit, so I can move on to the next step. The moment Dave moves the task in Trello to the completed column, I get a message in the project channel in Slack.

I was able to create a task for Dave and be told once Dave had completed it, without needing to call or email him or wonder when it had been done.

Once I'd created the task, I could get on with my day, without interruption, knowing there was complete transparency about the project and its progress.

Are you starting to see what a system like this can do inside your business? As scary as it may seem, embracing these tools and systems could be exactly what you need to help your existing team to reach the goals that seem to be just outside your reach and those that seem impossible to achieve with your existing setup.

# Conclusion

Now it's over to you!

I hope this book has inspired you to take your business by the scruff of the neck and get some proper systems and processes in place.

As I suggested at the start, the three systems should really be implemented in reverse.

Business owners are naturally drawn towards the front end of the customer journey: they want to generate new leads and find new customers as quickly as possible.

While this is understandable, it would be a big mistake to take that approach as you create the three key systems in your business.

Once you have a properly thought-through lead-generation system, you won't be able to function without properly planned and designed client-acquisition and client-fulfilment systems.

Because you picked up this book and have made it this far, I assume you already have a business and some existing customers. Use them to test and embed your newly designed client-fulfilment system. This will give you invaluable feedback on what works – and what doesn't – before you start driving more and more new clients into the system.

Also, be prepared to trip up on some of the details. You cannot foresee everything at the design stage. It is only when you start to use your system and get feedback from your team and your customers that you'll discover the gaps and shortfalls.

Don't be disheartened by this. Remember: unless you have a system, you can't improve it.

Whatever you do, please don't embark on this journey and then return to your old ways the moment something doesn't quite work.

Stay focussed on the big picture and the huge advantages to be gained from what you're designing and building.

**Take your team with you**

It is crucial for the success and long-term improvement of your systems and processes, and ultimately your business, that you have your team on board.

Lead from the front: make sure everyone is aware of how committed and dedicated you are to this new way of working. The moment you lose interest and your team senses it, they'll think it's just another idea from above which, if they can ignore it long enough, will be replaced with something else.

Make sure you involve the right members of your team in designing and executing this business re-engineering project. Everyone should know that they are taking part in shaping the future of your business and that you value their input and take it seriously. Don't just pay lip service to suggestions from your team. Remember, they work with the systems and processes every day and they might know more than you do.

**Meet challenges head on**

As you go from the exciting design phase of this project into the actual implementation, expect it to go through cycles of fast, visible progress and days when nothing seems to fall into place. Don't worry – this is normal.

All important work has elements of great frustration. Your most important role in redesigning your business is to push things forward and make sure some progress is made every day.

If you hit a tricky patch, don't abandon the project for a week or two to see what happens. You and your team will lose momentum and it will take much more energy to get things going again.

**Find a balance**

Finally, I encourage you to keep a balance between the micro and the macro elements of your systems and processes.

On the macro level, there are only five steps in the process of a kitchen-installation company:

1. Receive enquiry
2. Design kitchen
3. Order kitchen
4. Deliver kitchen
5. Install kitchen.

On the face of it, that's all there is to running a kitchen-installation company. But we both know it's a little more complex!

On the micro level, there are several steps between each of the five milestones listed above.

When implementing your three key systems, be aware of the macro and micro and be flexible about switching between them as required. Don't get buried in the minute steps that make up every action. By the same token, don't ignore the details in the pursuit of the easiest solution.

Always focus always on finding the right and best solution. That is, the right and best solution for **now**. You'll always be changing and improving your system as your business grows.

And it will!

Enjoy the journey.

# Acknowledgements

Firstly, I'd like to thank my two colleagues at Barefoot Digital, David Browne and Jean de Villiers (also my older brother). Working with the two of you every day has allowed me to focus on what is really important, challenges me to learn and grow every single day and allows me to share, every day, the world we are creating for ourselves.

My family, Sophie, Amélie and Olivia – this is all for you and because of you. From Mr Grumpy to Mr Happy, without the three of you, none of this would have felt possible.

Gryse Moeder, Oupa Jan, Babchia, Rayray, Grandad Bob – your help and support has been and continues to be invaluable to me.

Jean, Nicolette and Nico – from building bombs in the garden, Lego helicopters with cassette deck motors and all the crazy shit we got up to, to this. Always there, always helping, always inspiring.

Lucy McCarraher and Joe Gregory at RethinkPress – thank you for your complete support and incredible attention to detail. Without you and your team, this book would still just be an idea and a few scribbled notes.

Daniel Priestley and everyone at Dent. You guys play a different game and gave me a completely new perspective on my business and what I want to achieve.

Nigel Botterill and everyone I've met over the years at the Entrepreneurs Circle. The inspiration and support I get from all of you, being able to help where I can and seeing fellow entrepreneurs achieve their goals is a source of inspiration I couldn't imagine being without.

Michael E. Gerber – for your books, inspiration, ongoing guidance and a single day that is turning an idea into a business.

The Awesome. You guys know exactly what it has taken for this book to be a reality, and your friendship, advice, support and inspiration continues the journey.

Janke – at 16-years-old, you badgered me into reading a book for the first time. Now, you can read mine.

# The Author

Pieter K de Villiers is a small-business marketing and systems specialist.

Born and raised in South Africa, Pieter first came to the UK in 1997.

Having started his first business in 2005, Pieter first started developing systems and processes for his own business, and over the next decade learnt exactly what it takes to move a business from a one-man-band to a growing business, with repeat customers and predictable growth.

In 2014, realising a real opportunity in the market, Pieter started Barefoot Funnels, helping countless small businesses develop and implement the three key systems every small business needs to help them to realise the potential they have, often allowing them to double their output without the need for additional staff.

In 2015, Pieter joined forces with Jean de Villiers and David Browne to form Barefoot Digital, focussing on creating and setting up the three key systems in small business as well as a complete digital marketing solution for a select number of clients.

You can contact Pieter at:

email: pieter@barefoot-digital.com

Twitter: @pkdevilliers

Facebook: www.facebook.com/pieter.devilliers.5

www.barefoot-digital.com or www.pieterkdevilliers.com